little chickin's name

given by

A

seed factory

collaborative

FARM GRUB™

A to Z

Adapted from the original cloth book
with a Special Section for Grown Peeps

―――――――――

tips for 'growing
healthy kids
from **scratch**'™

FARMER GOAT favors...

Asparagus

Broccoli

Carrots

Dinosaur kale

™

LIL' CHICKIN likes...

Endive

Fennel

Grapes

Haricots verts

LA VACA loves...

Ice cream

Jicama

Kiwi

Lime

DUCKIE desires...

Melon

Nectarines

Okra

Parsnips

™

HORSE hankers for...

Quinoa

Rutabagas

Squash

Tomatoes

PIGGLES prefers...

Udon noodles

Vichyssoise

Watermelon   and...

Xtra **Y**ummy **Z**ucchinis!

Won't YOU try...

• **amaranth** • barley • buckwheat • bulgur • corn • millet • oats • quinoa

• rice • rye • wheat • **artichokes** • arugula • asparagus • bamboo shoots

• basil • bay leaves • bibb lettuce • black beans • beets • black-eyed peas

• broccoli • brussel sprouts • boston lettuce • butternut squash • cabbage

• carrots • cassava • celery • chickpeas • cilantro • collard greens

• coriander • corn • cucumber • dandelion greens • dill • eggplant • endive

• escarole • fennel • field greens • garbanzo beans • ginger • green leaf

lettuce • green onions • green peppers • red leaf lettuce • romaine

• radiccio • kale • watercress • spinach • grape leaf • jerusalem artichoke

• jicama • kohlrabi • kidney beans • leeks • lemongrass • lentils • lima

beans • mint • mushrooms • mustard greens • navy beans • okra • olives

• onions • oregano • palm hearts • parsley • parsnips • peas • pinto

beans • potatoes • pumpkin • red beans • red radish • rhubarb

• rosemary • rutabaga • sage • scallions • seaweed • soybeans (a.k.a edamame) • acorn squash • spaghetti squash • Swiss chard • taro • tarragon • tomatillo • tomato • turnip • turnip greens • water chestnut • white beans • yellow squash • zuchhini • **apple** • apricot • avocado • banana • blackberry • blueberry • cantaloupe • cherry • cranberry • date • dragonfruit • fig • grapefruit • grapes • guava • honeydew melon • jackfruit • kiwi • kumquat • lemon • lime • loganberry • loquat • mango • muscadines • nectarines • oranges • papaya • peaches • pears • persimmon • pineapple • plantain • plum • pomegranate • pomelo • prune • tangerine • watermelon • **almond milk** • buttermilk • cheeses • cow milk • cream • eggnog • frozen yogurt • goat milk • ice cream • kefir • milkshake • pudding • rice milk • sheep milk • sour cream • soy milk • yogurt • **fish** (so many yummy kinds - look for sustainably harvested fish) • meat (go for lean meats if you eat them • beans! (legumes) • eggs • nuts (including nut butters) • seeds & more ... EXPLORE!

Guess who?...

FARMER GOAT

LIL' CHICKIN

LA VACA

Who favors broccoli?

Who likes grapes?

Who loves kiwi?

DUCKIE

HORSE

PIGGLES

Who desires nectarines?

Who hankers for tomatoes?

Who prefers watermelon?

Special Section for Grown Peeps

tips for growing
healthy kids
from scratch

(for grown peeps)

TIP 1   Start with food culture…

Building a healthy food culture in your home is essential for raising healthy kids
(or "little chickins" as we like to call them)

Talking positively about healthy foods and **building a healthy "food vocabulary"** from an early age are two great ways to build a healthy food culture in your coop!

Start with a game … play **FIND, BUY & TRY**

Take **FARM GRUB AtoZ** to the market.

- **FIND** the foods listed in the book. Talk about what type of foods they are: VEGGIES? FRUITS? and where they came from: BELOW THE GROUND? IN A TREE?

- **BUY** some and prepare (use a familiar preparation if possible)

- Then everybody* **TRY** it! (Grown Peeps, make sure you set a good example)
  *Make sure new foods are age appropriate and that your kids are not allergic to them.

You may have to serve new foods several different times or ways before they are accepted, but don't give up.

Eating a wide variety of healthy foods is one of the best ways to ensure that your little chickins are getting all the nutrients they need!

FARM GRUB AtoZ is a great tool to build a healthy food culture in your coop! Enjoy and Keep on Cluckin'

– Mother Hen

TIP 2   Buy locally grown food …

There are many places to get the food we eat.
• Grocery stores have lots of food • Restaurants have it too…

But **FARMER GOAT** would love you to get more food straight from a **local** farm. That might be your own garden or one down the road just a little bit…

Why is eating local food important?
Because buying food that is grown close to your home means it's going to be fresher and more nutritious for your body.

Buying food from local farmers also keeps them in business. Subscribing to a Community Supported Agriculture share (CSA) will get you a regular box of food straight from the farm! It also allows farmers to know that the food they grow **will** be sold.

Buying food from local farmers is more fun! Find a local Farmers' Market and visit regularly. Get to know the farmers. Ask them why they farm and about their food – they are proud of it and love to talk about it.

Visit farms where you can pick your own seasonal treats like strawberries, blueberries, pumpkins and such. Make finding healthy food fun!

TIP 3   Support healthy food systems…

Healthy Food Systems are ones that support sustainable growing practices, local food distribution systems and generally build great communities around healthy, REAL FOOD.

Find more about what's going on
with your local food scene here!
www.localharvest.org
www.slowfoodusa.org

And **support organizations** that work
to promote Healthy Food Systems in your community
like these near our coop in Atanta, GA

www.georgiaorganics.org   www.slowfoodatlanta.org   www.atlantalocalfood.org

GEORGIA ORGANICS
GOOD FOOD FOR ALL

Slow Food Atlanta
slowfoodatlanta.org

TIP 4   Make a list …

A few new foods to try soon:

_____

- _____
_____
_____

- _____
_____
_____

- _____
_____
_____

- _____
_____
_____

- _____
_____

New places to shop for food:
local farmers market, nearby farms, ethnic grocery stores, etc.

_____

- _____
_____
_____

- _____
_____

Fun food field trips to take:
farms with u-pick berries (go organic!), a local dairy, a chicken coop tour, etc.

_____

- _____
_____
_____

- _____
_____

TIP 5 Listen up!...

Reading and repeating the **FARM GRUB AtoZ's** will familiarize young children with the alphabet AND new foods.

But the FARM GRUB team took "the power of audible learning" one step further with a wonderful CD chock-full of **"catchy tunes 'bout healthy stuff for the whole family."**

Check out these fun tunes • REAL FOOD • Snackcake Blues • Tango Empanada • Duckie's Nag •Lamentation for the Rotten Zuchini & more.

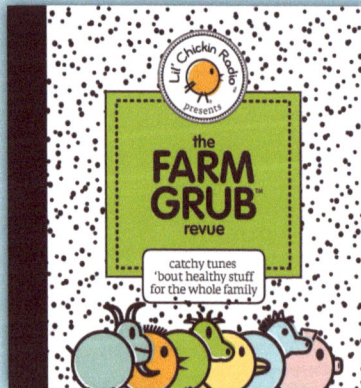

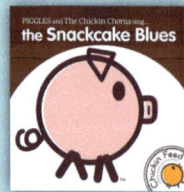

Lil' Chickin Radio presents the full CD of tunes and singles available for download too.

For songs and downloadable fun stuff www.chickinfeed.com/farm-grub

TIP 6   Find more good stuff here…

www.chickinfeed.com

twitter facebook blog

Peep out!

www.ingramcontent.com/pod-product-compliance
Lightning Source LLC
Chambersburg PA
CBHW041557040426
42447CB00002B/211